CLUTCHING MY PEARLS!

Why Marketing for Small Businesses Doesn't Work and What Will

Bruce Prins

COPYRIGHT © 2022 Bruce Prins

Book Cover Designed by Craig Prins © 2022

Cover images curtesy of Pixabay.com and Cleanpng.com

The content contained within this book may not be reproduced, duplicated or transmitted without direct written permission from the author.

Under no circumstances will any blame or legal responsibility be held against the author, for any damages, reparation, or monetary loss due to the information contained within this book, either directly or indirectly.

Legal Notice:

This book is copyright protected. It is only for personal use. You cannot amend, distribute, sell, use, quote or paraphrase any part, or the content within this book, without the consent of the author.

Disclaimer Notice:

Please note the information contained within this document is for educational and entertainment purposes only. All effort has been executed to present accurate, up-to-date, reliable, complete information. No warranties of any kind are declared or implied.

By reading this document, the reader agrees that under no circumstances is the author responsible for any losses, direct or indirect, that are incurred as a result of the use of the information contained within this document, including, but not limited to, errors, omissions, or inaccuracies.

TABLE OF CONTENTS

About the Author v
INTRODUCTION 1
CHAPTER 1: WHAT IS MARKETING? 8
    Approach 8
    Conduct 10
    Planning 11
    Measurements 14

CHAPTER 2: CONTEMPORARY MARKETING 17
    Modern Marketing 17
    Does It Work? 24

CHAPTER 3: WHAT IS SALES? 26
    Definition 26
    Tactics 28
    Information 30
    Changes 34
    Sales Techniques 37

CHAPTER 4: QUALITY IS EVERYTHING 50
    Definition 50
    Importance 51

CHAPTER 5: WHAT IS CONSISTENCY? 62
    Align Your Efforts 64

Define Your Brand 64
Keep Your Plans 65
Review Your Results 65
Moving Forward 66

CHAPTER 6: IT TAKES A VILLAGE 67

Importance 69
Development 71
Involvement 72
Finding a Community 75

CHAPTER 7: WORD-OF-MOUTH 77

Definition 78
Importance 81
Strategies 83
Benefit Your Business 88

CHAPTER 8: HAVE SOME STANDARDS 90

Definition 91
Purpose 91
Control 93
Implement 94

CONCLUSION 96
REFERENCES 101

ABOUT THE AUTHOR

Bruce Prins, MBA, is a Certified Management Consultant, Occupational Development Practitioner, and Modern Applied Psychologist. He also holds numerous IT management and software qualifications and is a member of the Mensa high-IQ society.

For over 30 years, he has worked within the hospitality, education, healthcare, fashion, IT, and retail industries. He started his career as a cleaner in a cinema and eventually became a Chief Executive of a hospital group. He currently freelances as a Coach, Mentor, Author, and Consultant.

Bruce, a proud father of a disabled teenager and an accomplished artist, loves writing and enjoys history, cinema, various television genres, and reading romantic, historical, or fantasy fiction.

INTRODUCTION

There's a multitude of small businesses everywhere you look. They range from the local mom-and-pop convenience store to the nearest independent hotel. There are pensioners running a market stall, freelance photographers, independent authors, and people offering services from painting your house to fixing your garden furniture. It's glaringly apparent that entrepreneurs are trying to make a living no matter in which country you find them in.

Now, how do they get new customers? It's here where marketing comes in. Marketing involves actively promoting your product or service using advertising, awareness, and promotion techniques. It's about getting people to know what you do or sell, why they should pay for it, and where to get it.

So why the title of this book? We'll get to the specifics later because there's much you first need to understand or be reminded of. Still, it's possible for the marketing to work for you to some extent. How you approach marketing currently may be ineffective and probably a waste of money. In fact, what you consider great marketing strategies primarily benefit large multinational companies with enormous budgets.

Otherwise, you'd have no idea of many of the big sports, clothing, food, and beverage brands out there. You wouldn't be aware of the latest movie or what you can watch on streaming. If you desperately need more sales, marketing gurus will tell you the many reasons for your failure. So, let's dive into these possible reasons first.

You may be diversifying too much. Instead of sticking with one or a few products, you're trying to appeal to too many people. The same can be said if you're offering services that are too generalized, such as house maintenance. Think about it, if you needed some painting, wouldn't you prefer to hire a painter than get the local handyman to do the work? Seriously, does this handyman know enough about house painting, or is it just something he can do amongst other things? He'd probably do it the same way you would if you decided to paint the house yourself.

It doesn't mean you can't add products or services to what you're already offering, but first, get your business going before doing so. The same goes for increasing the size of the area where your products or services are available. Instead, focus on what area or region you realistically can service and then, if you have enough money, expand into other areas. It could be either physically or virtually.

The thing is that you'll face a multitude of problems if you try to simultaneously offer new products or services to multiple markets.

It'll make your marketing efforts more expensive and increase production and distribution costs. This is besides spreading you thin when trying to keep all your customers happy. Worse still is if you think your marketing is aimed at the best-suited potential customers when it isn't.

So many different marketing strategies exist but let's look at a few major ones.

- With customary marketing, you focus on promoting your brand using electronic media (radio, television) or printed media (newspapers, flyers, billboards).
- Outbound marketing is where you're cold-calling on potential customers by either visiting them in person or sending them unsolicited emails.
- When it comes to inbound marketing, you try and entice potential customers to contact you using content marketing, where you're focused on publishing and distributing content online for a specific audience.
- Digital marketing is where you leverage online tools, such as social media boosting campaigns, search engine optimization, and online advertisements.
- Event marketing involves using events to attract and reach potential customers.

So many more strategies are available for you to apply but note that something that worked a decade ago doesn't necessarily work today.

In addition, digital and event marketing has become the preferred strategies of late, especially for small businesses or freelancers. It doesn't mean the others don't work since you still see the large fast food chains using them, amongst others.

Some of your efforts will reach your intended audience, while others won't. If they do, some customers may not find any appeal in what you're offering or receive the wrong impression. Some aspects of your products or services might've connected with your target market in the past but could have no effect these days.

One of the fundamental rules of selling a product or service is meeting a need. So, before they buy, the customer looks at what they'll benefit from, not how good your product or services are. If you focus on the features and not the benefits of your product or service when you're promoting the latter, you'll lose the potential customer. And it will be even better if you have customer reviews or images showing what you've accomplished than simply telling them how good you are.

Now, you may ask if it isn't crucial for a potential customer to know your products' features upfront. It isn't. They need to believe your product fulfills a need to attract them as a customer. Then, to decide to be and remain a customer, they need to agree to its features and how it satisfies their needs. The latter builds credibility with your customers.

Another reason your marketing efforts may fail is because you lack clarification on who your target market is and what they're looking for. You must show your target market that you understand what they're looking for and that you've just got the product or service that will solve their problems or meet their needs. Then, anytime you want to market your business, you need to know where you see it going, how you plan to get there, and who your customers are and will be. Then you choose a marketing strategy and plan your next steps. But remember, you need to know if you can handle increased customer demand while offering your existing customers the best products or services you can deliver.

Astoundingly, some businesses still need to identify and know their target market. Often, a company or freelancer targets people by location, region, or the fact that they might be interested. This leads to a waste of money spent on promotions and sales efforts. You must define your target market as who they are, where they are, what they value, and why they'd need or want your product or service. The message won't be persuasive if you send generic messages about your offering to the general market.

Don't be everything to everyone; don't focus on what makes you special. Instead, focus on five unique things you can do better than your competitors and provide these with consistency and quality all the time. The latter will be associated with your brand and be seen as your value proposition (what you can do for or provide to others).

An important area where small businesses or service providers often fail is not following up on requests, messages, calls, or complaints. Sometimes it's not intentional and could be because they don't check all their communication channels frequently. Often, small businesses get messages via social media applications but rarely read or respond to them. It's because they prefer dealing with customers in front of them than worrying about past or potential customers. That's a big no-no and will cost you dearly regarding reputation damage and loss in potential sales. Also, if you proactively follow up on a proposal you sent or a likely lead that was supposed to get back to you, you'll possibly make a sale.

Though the marketing gurus have a point, you only sometimes have the resources, time, or ability to do successful marketing. In addition, the way the world works is that your small enterprise's visibility is a threat to any larger competitor that meets a similar need for customers. As soon as your business succeeds and grows, a more significant business, locally or nationally, will likely want to buy you out. They could then operate your business as it is, absorb it into theirs, or even delete your brand from the market. The latter would entail simply incorporating your customer base and adding your product or service to their catalog.

Of course, the prospect of a more significant business buying you out could be appealing.

Interestingly though, most of the time, these businesses wouldn't but instead target the products or services you're successfully selling by undercutting you in price and delivery proficiency. Even if it means they lose money doing so. The point is to quickly put you out of business, reinstate their price, and add your customers to their market share. It may seem surprising, but it's true. There's no morality in capitalism.

So, what are your options, then? There are a few, and they'll be explored in this book. You should walk away by the end of the book, having a better understanding of what you haven't been doing, what you're wasting your efforts and money on, and what you should focus on instead.

CHAPTER 1: WHAT IS MARKETING?

Marketing is any effort you make to communicate your product and services to potential customers. These potential customers are referred to as your target market. In other words, the people you want to buy or pay for your products or services. They have to know you exist and what you can offer or do for them, and the process of letting them know is called marketing.

To know who your market is and whether they need what you're offering them, you must conduct market research. It's where you identify who your customer is, why they're your customer, and how you'll be able to interact with them. Letting them know who you are, requires you to have a "brand." If you aren't using your own name, your "brand" is then the name, design, or symbol that potential customers will identify your business with.

Approach

The approach you take to market yourself to your potential customers is called a marketing strategy. There are many, and a few were alluded to in the introduction. In the next chapter we'll focus on contemporary or modern strategies.

For now, you need to know that an effective way of approaching any marketing strategy you employ is to look at specific areas you should focus on. If you're selling a product, you should consider what's referred to as the four "Ps."

- What Product or service are you selling, and is it clearly packaged or presented?
- What is your selling Price, and is it competitive and realistic?
- At what Place will you be selling the product or providing your services?
- How will you Promote yourself, your product, or your service and how will your offering be branded, advertised, and introduced to your target market?

If you're providing a service, you should consider an additional four "Ps" when working on your marketing strategy.

- Who are the People who'll be providing these services, and what are their competencies (you or maybe your staff)?
- What Process will you apply for providing the service in having customers request and you deliver such service?
- What Physical evidence will there be that you've delivered the service?

- What Promise will you make so your customer is assured that your service will be done correctly, ethically, and in line with their expectations?

Let's add another "P." What Perception will you create by providing your product or services? In other words, what will your target market perceive and then value about what you've provided them with?

Any marketing message creates an impression and an expectation with a potential customer. Thus, when drafting a marketing strategy, it isn't just about putting the message out there but also ensuring the right message is communicated by you. You want to try your best to ensure your message is interpreted correctly by potential customers.

Conduct

When marketing your business, remember that some countries have strict laws that ensure you don't act dishonestly toward customers. You should investigate the ones that apply to you, but here are a few generic ones to abide by.

- Don't mislead a customer.
- Don't make defamatory comments about your competition.
- Respect your customer's privacy and personal information.

- Don't commit fraud.
- Don't use another business' brands or intellectual property without their permission.
- Don't extort sponsorship or loyalty.

Remember to never misrepresent yourself, your products, or your services. You could be criminally charged or even become financially liable.

Planning

Regardless of the marketing strategy you employ, you probably have activities you want to undertake to attract potential customers. Obviously, you have to plan your activities ahead of time. To do so, you need to consider the following for every action you undertake.

- What is your reason for doing this activity?
- Who are you aiming to attract?
- When will the activity take place?
- What steps or actions will the activity consist of?
- How much will it cost?
- Where will the activity take place?
- How will you measure the effectiveness of the activity?

The four management principles are to plan, organize, lead and control. By applying these four principles to everything, you can achieve what you aim for.

If you remain hands-on, learn from your mistakes, ask for advice, and remember what works, you should accomplish a lot.

It goes without saying that you want to increase sales. So, when estimating potential revenue from your marketing activities, consulting with others in your area or industry is essential. It's important because you'll need to keep yourself abreast of what's happening in your environment and market since it can affect your business. Examples of these effects could be holidays, changes in banking regulations, or even the cancellation of a local big sporting event or concert. It depends on your business and how these effects will impact your supply of products or services.

Of course, suppose you've been at your business for a long time and keep yourself informed through the media. In that case, you'd have developed a "feel" for potential sales opportunities and what efforts you could employ to increase sales. And to maximize your sales targets, you'll need to often review or improve the targets you've set up. You'll have to consider whether your aim is to maximize revenue based on value or price. If your price is low, you'll get more sales, or are you of the opinion that you'll instead have a high price and try for more customers? It depends on the type of product or service you offer and what your competition does. It's up to you.

Promotional activities are successful if you've achieved your sales targets, completed your desired objectives, and retained new-found customers. Receiving positive feedback from the latter would also endorse your efforts.

But, when creating your marketing plan, follow the key steps below:

1. draft your plan
2. communicate the plan with your team if you have staff
3. monitor the implementation of your plan
4. evaluate the plan's effectiveness
5. make adjustments if necessary
6. continue to implement, monitor, and evaluate the plan as time goes on
7. review the end result of the period you've chosen

If you have a team, when presenting your plan to them, remember to have your presentation structured. The presentation can start with an introduction, state the objectives, including the actual plan and implementation method, and then have a conclusion, highlighting your team's role in achieving your objectives and the review criteria that will be used.

It would help if you also briefed your team about your proposed marketing activities by focusing on the following content.

- Brief your team on the product or service being promoted.
- Brief your team on the interrelationship between the products being promoted and your products or services.
- Brief your team on what products need to be promoted by your team to increase sales.

Planning helps you focus on the steps you need to make your business successful and enables you to achieve your objectives.

Measurements

Any marketing strategy or promotion activity is only effective if you and your team are motivated to improve sales and achieve your targets. You can encourage your team by reminding them of the benefits of the business's longevity. Consider linking incentives to the targets you've set for them. Just be careful because once an incentive is implemented, it may be difficult to remove the continued expectation for incentives in the future.

At the same time as motivating your team, you should monitor the effectiveness of every promotional activity. As an example, you may offer a discounted deal to customers. Then see how much of that discounted product or service has generated revenue. Don't forget to check if those same customers who bought your discounted offer didn't also pay for some of your other products or services at the same time.

Another way is to compare your customer feedback to the actual sales generated. Also, scrutinize your costs to determine that your plan isn't damaging your profitability and sustainability. In other words, it costs so much that your business can't meet its obligations.

There's a considerable difference between evaluating and reviewing. Evaluating is a continuous process where reviewing is only done at the end of an exercise to see if it effectively achieved its objectives. So when considering your sales activities, it's essential to adjust the factors within the plan to better achieve your targets. Sometimes, your targets must be reviewed to make them more realistic.

However, the most critical measure of the success of a promotional or sales activity is your customers' feedback. This feedback will give you a good indication of what your customers think or have experienced when participating in the activity, which could have been conscious or unconscious.

Remember to respect all feedback, even if it seems irrelevant or uninformed. If a customer has their facts wrong, they should have been informed correctly.

Future sales should always be planned based on current results. It creates a more realistic expectation and can encourage the desired growth you need to achieve to improve the performance of your enterprise.

Compare apples with apples and pears with pears. It doesn't help to compare January 2021 with June 2022. It's unrealistic. When planning your year's targets, use the previous year as a reference for the coming or current year. It will be more relevant in context than if a period from over a decade ago is used to determine your current expectation.

And remember, you represent your business, whether positively or negatively, at all times.

CHAPTER 2: CONTEMPORARY MARKETING

Contemporary marketing strategies focus on the customer instead of the market. Simply put, it's where you focus your marketing on individuals instead of groups of similar people. It means that the products and services you sell are more varied to try and meet individual preferences. Though this goes against what is stated in the introduction, where the emphasis was that you specialize, the differential here is that the current focus above is suited to larger businesses. As a small business, you need more resources and practical capacity to cater to many needs.

Modern Marketing

But let's still investigate what these modern strategies are. They offer your customers a choice. Your target market has a wide range of products promoted toward them, depending on their desires instead of what you want them to have.

In the old days, you would attract customers back to you by ensuring parts of what you supply needed replenishment or replacement. It was an effective strategy, and some companies continue to do this. But, these days, it's more difficult because customers have become more intelligent and spoilt for choice. They can do research before they decide to buy your product.

They often need to avoid falling into the trap of being tied to your product due to future needs to maintain their use of it.

Gamification

One of the contemporary marketing strategies aims to create a connection between you and your customer through gamification. It's where you inspire your customers to engage with you by using games or learning valuable skills or obtaining information. It can even include entertainment.

An example would be aligning your chili sauce business with a recipe book so customers can buy your sauce and cook it at home. As a small business, that could work if you're handing out recipes. Still, to truly make it effective, you would have to link them to popular recipes and chefs, requiring you to pay the authors royalties or fees for the chefs' time. Never mind that you'd still have to spend marketing funds promoting it online.

Though it seems like a great idea, how would your small business cope with what's required to manage such a co-creation program? Though it would definitely entice more customers, think of the money involved.

Shared Value

Another contemporary strategy is to develop value sharing for your customer. Suppose you're selling unique bedding, but you also offer a far reduced laundry service for that bedding. It could be after you've negotiated this partnership with the laundromat in town or you decided to open your own to serve your customers. It may sound excessive, but it does show you what shared value can do for a potential customer. Again, do you have the resources and network to organize such a solution for your customers?

Influencers

With an influencer marketing strategy, you leverage your brand onto an individual who has influence over potential customers who, in most cases, are their online social media followers. You could create activities or events around said influencer to drive your brand message to their followers.

But you'll have to fork out a lot of cash for this. The more prominent the influencer, the more expensive they are. They're usually celebrities, business leaders, fitness gurus, content creators, customer advocates, etc.

Connecting

A relationship marketing strategy refers to segmenting your potential customers to build loyalty.

You rely on databases, advertising aimed at online behavior, and targeted customer analytics. You can imagine the costs involved in accessing this information and then using it to market your products and services.

Going Viral

Viral marketing will encourage your followers, hopefully, your customers online, to pass along your advertising message. The term "viral" means that something has moved across social media platforms and channels like a virus, reaching millions. That's if you're lucky. Getting the same for your small business is more difficult than you think because a large amount of entertainment value is needed. Many people are drawn to what entertains or creates a strong emotional response in them. If you have an influencer on payroll, then it could happen. But, once again, you're looking at large amounts of cash, which your small business may need help to afford.

Using Keywords

The all-popular keyword marketing strategy involves placing a message in front of your potential customers based on the keywords and phrases they're using to search for products or services online. The main advantage of this strategy is that you can reach the right people with the right message at the right time. For many marketers, this involves the placement of an advertisement containing specific keywords.

Using keywords is an excellent method to advertise online. It's proving very popular because it attracts people searching for a product or service using particular words to hopefully locate your business. Yet again, it costs money to advertise online, and then there are often charges levied at you by the number of times someone "clicks" on your business profile, product or service. Even if they don't end up buying or paying for it.

Search Engine Optimization

Search engine optimization (SEO) is where you try and improve your product or service's visibility when people use search engines. You have to see it in two ways. First, it involves how your website, if you have one, is indexed on the major search engines and includes the right keywords, content, and links. Secondly, you select specific keywords that allow your website to appear at the top or close to it when people do searches.

The above can be achieved by ensuring your website aligns well with the search engine algorithms. It's about ranking. For example, when you type the word "cinema" in the search engine, you'll notice that specific sites are listed first and are often always the same. They have spent the money on expertise to have their websites indexed well and contain the right keywords. When using search engines to advertise your website, you'll also pay per "click." It does sound great and is effective for many businesses.

But, again, it excludes the capacity of the average small business or entrepreneur. Though you could do it cheaply enough you may not get the attention you're looking for and thus waste money.

Content Marketing

Now let's look at content marketing. It's where you create and share valuable and consistent content to attract a specific audience. Your aim is to solicit customers who'll spend money as a result. You're using the story associated with you and your brand to endear yourself and your products or services to potential customers. This can cost a lot of money because you need content creators, a platform where you can place the content, and the means to promote said content to the world.

Boosting

The boosting marketing strategy is done on social media. It's prevalent amongst small businesses and individual freelancers. It can be done quickly enough, and you can spend less than the more expensive marketing strategies.

It's a popular marketing strategy because of the following.

- It cost-effectively reaches your target audience when compared to more expensive options.
- It increases brand awareness for you on social media.

- It allows you to collect usage statistics for your next marketing strategy.

But before you get excited, let's first delve into what it is and how it works. When you boost your post on social media, you pay the platform to show one of your posts to your followers and targeted audience. The platform may suggest a recommended audience based on your profile. Still, you can target areas and specific profiles and interests of your intended audience. Your post will then be labeled as "sponsored" on others' feeds.

Of course, it isn't free. You have to specify a budget you're willing to spend on the boosting campaign. This you do by selecting how many days you want your campaign to run and how many of your targeted audience you wish to reach each day. The more money you're willing to spend per day, the more potential customers you'll gain. Well, that's what they tell you.

In reality, the algorithms are not that cut and dry. For example, suppose you're not operating in the country where the social media platform is based. In that case, the likelihood of reaching that country's audience, if you intentionally wish to, is reduced substantially. Even if you paid for it. The social media platform prefers to promote you to your local audience.

Though they tell you afterward how many views, clicks and likes you received, many booster campaigns need more interaction from potential customers.

Even when your budget is substantial. In fact, a lot of the time, the only return on investment is job applications or unsolicited messages known as "spam" sent to your inbox. In addition, other small businesses will comment on your boosted post to piggyback on your campaign for their marketing efforts. Worse still is that you disappear from your target audience's feeds as soon as your campaign is done until you try again. You'd have to do a booster campaign for weeks or months to build awareness while changing your boosted posts often to avoid potential customers getting bored.

It's true that for big businesses or wealthier entrepreneurs, social media boosting campaigns can work amazingly. It's in their best interest to push their access to audiences as long as they're prepared to spend millions. Social media is prevalent these days, and these large booster campaigns are why we're inundated with advertisements on our social media feeds. It now comes at the cost of failing to see our friends' recent posts or updates.

Does It Work?

Traditional and contemporary marketing have their distinct advantages and disadvantages. The former works well for larger companies who want to diversify their products or services. Thus, attracting customers to their products or services rather than their brand.

Whereas businesses that use contemporary strategies aim to build a loyal relationship with their customers. You can use elements of both, but it will still cost you money. A lot of it.

After all, is said and done, the issue is whether your marketing expense is justified by the actual profit you generate. It's here that there's a gap between what you're taught marketing can do for you compared to whether it can really get you the sales you need. Emulating what works for big business is what's wrong with this picture. Sure, there are strategies mentioned you could do on a smaller scale hoping for that significant return on your investment. Still, there are other things you can do to promote your business, but more on that later.

CHAPTER 3: WHAT IS SALES?

Sales are an essential factor in helping your small business grow. It appears apparent, but often, it's only seen as taking cash from a customer in exchange for supplying them with a product or service. Understanding what sales entail is vital to make the most out of every transaction. Whether it be for financial gain or reputation enhancement.

Definition

Often people confuse sales with marketing even though they're distinctively different. While marketing promotes your product to potential customers, sales refer to exchanging a product or service for money. It involves you helping potential customers by listening to them and understanding their wants and needs. Instead of persuading them to pay for your product or service, selling focuses on objectively meeting their needs.

So, what's selling in simple terms? Selling is the transfer of money for a product or service while highlighting the latter's benefits and usefulness to a customer.

Selling skills refer to traits that make someone a good salesperson.

These skills are developed over time with experience, training, and coaching. It may include being able to conduct the selling process, which consists of the following steps:

1. Identify a prospective customer.
2. Prepare a catalog or supporting information.
3. Approach a potential customer.
4. Present a product or service to the potential customer.
5. Overcome any objections they may have.
6. Close the sale and conduct the financial transaction.
7. Follow up on whether they're satisfied or need something more.

The skills above should also include upselling and add-on selling.

- Upselling is where you suggest a more expensive product or service to a potential customer than they chose. The benefits to the customer have to be evident for them to take the more expensive option.
- Add-on selling is when you suggest a product or service that could complement their chosen selection to better meet their needs. Thus making a more significant sale.

Both of these approaches have to occur during the actual transaction because they're difficult to do after the fact.

Tactics

Selling a product or service can happen in various ways. It depends on the approach you take. Below are a few methods you could consider.

- If you take an aggressive approach, you'll try to make a sale by convincing your customers why they need your product or service and how they would benefit from doing so. You may even include a special deal linked to a limited time frame.
- With a transactional approach, you focus on a customer's needs and make the sale as quickly as possible. In actual fact, the customer already knows what they want when they approach you. Instead of spending time understanding what the customer really needs, you focus on making a quick sale. You should know that sometimes customers think what they're buying is meeting their needs, where often it might be a different match. Just be aware of that since you could help the customer get what they really need. Remember, all of us don't know what we don't know, and you can't expect your customer to know something they probably won't unless you tell them.
- If you apply a social approach, you target potential customers directly through social media.

- When taking a needs-oriented approach, you get to know your customer's needs by asking them questions that will allow you to offer them a better solution.

If you decide to hire staff to assist you with selling your product or service, you should know the types of sales roles there are. It will aid you in determining which are the best suited to your business.

- A sales associate's job is encouraging customers to buy your product directly.
- A sales representative sells your products or services to prospective businesses and organizations. If they work inside your premises, they focus on interacting with your customers via mobile, email, or when the latter shows up. If they're allowed to visit customers, they may work from home and then make face-to-face sales visits to your customers. Either way, their role is to maintain a favorable business transaction and relationship in the hopes of making future sales.
- A Sales manager oversees a team of salespeople within a business. They use their leadership skills to set goals and support and mentor each member of your sales team. This role is usually found in a medium-to-large business unless your business is distribution or dealer-based. Then you'll have many sales personnel to interact with customers.

- A sales director supervises and manages a group of sales managers. This is usually a role in a large corporate organization.

How do you know if you or your salespeople are good at selling? It all depends on whether you or your team have the right skills. The following skills and traits are required to be a good salesperson.

- If you display empathy towards your customers, you're more likely to make a sale. Empathy helps you establish trust and shows respect from your side.
- If you're determined, it assists you with accomplishing your goals and sales targets. Determination helps you stay focused, thus leading to more sales.
- If you believe in yourself and the products or services you're selling, you'd be more apt to land a sale and make customers trust you and want to buy more from you in the future.

Remember, you can only sell what you believe in.

Information

It would help if you had a database containing the details of all your customers, including their contact information and purchase history. And you'll do well to have a database of potential customers you have come into contact with.

Include their contact details and the product or service you feel best suits them.

The main benefit of having a database of your existing customers is that you don't have to repeatedly ask for information or their history with your business. It shows professionalism and proves you care about their patronage.

Databases are beneficial for marketing and statistical purposes. Even if you think promoting your business to potential customers is essential, remember your existing customers. You can quickly lose track of them and then quietly lose them over the long term to your competitors. Examples of the information required on a customer database may include:

- the name of the customer or company or the company's representative
- the address of the customer
- the products or services the customer paid for
- the customer's personal identity or passport number (in some countries, this is mandatory)
- the customer's contact numbers
- the customer's e-mail addresses
- unique aspects of the customer in so far as special requests or preferences

Besides having a great database, you must ensure good communication between you and your team.

You can't assume that your team should know about it when you change a product or service, change a price, or implement a discount strategy. You have to ensure you communicate these changes to your team.

Sharing means informing and discussing the reasons for any changes so that your team can explain them adequately to a customer. If a customer asks, "Why has the price gone up again?" a team member can respond, "We continue to ensure our product meets the required quality levels. To do so, we've had to accommodate an increase in the cost of materials." They could also respond with, "Unfortunately, inflation has compelled us to review our pricing due to a rise in operating costs."

Once you have a product or service in place, it will be difficult to remove or cease to offer it, especially if it is popular with your customers. Suppose the availability of supplies or equipment causes the removal of a product or service. In that case, you can inform the customer: "The coffee makers are no longer available because we've had repeated problems with their longevity. We feel it's inconvenient for our customers to return them for repairs. We can, however, recommend our new coffee-pod machines." If it involves discontinuing a technical service, you can state, "We don't have the expertise in place any longer to offer that service but can suggest an alternative."

When it comes to selling, your business should have official policies documented. Whatever these are, they must be adhered to when selling a product or service to a customer. These policies may apply to:

- the limitations on discounted prices given to customers, staff, or groups.
- the conditions of payments to secure services or appointments
- the rules around how free products or services are provided to customers or staff
- how sales are recorded on your computer system or point of sales
- customer information is confidential within the constraints of the law
- how competitors aren't to be insulted
- how no promises are made that contradict the policies and standards of your business
- Etc.

Other policies that should be considered are:

- how extra services are provided
- no acceptance of bribes or gifts by staff to break the rules or add extra services
- how to avoid lying to customers about products or services

- not allowing customers access to areas, equipment, or inventory not offered as part of the product or services they're paying or have paid for

It would help if you also had an official refund or cancellation of service policy, considering who authorizes such and in what circumstances you do so. Keep a record of all refunds or cancellations to refer to in the future. It will also enable you to determine if customers are abusing your refund or cancellation policy.

Changes

Because your business will experience an increase in costs as time goes on, the need will arise where you'll have to increase your prices or rates. These price increases should happen after much thought has been put into the possible consequences. They could be because of a rise in costs, wages, taxes and other demands placed on your business.

Even though a customer may not be happy with a price increase, they should be aware of your careful consideration before doing so. Price is determined by costs, demand, inflation (i.e., the increase in the average price for goods), and the need to make a profit. Remember that you're running a business, not a charity.

Similar to price changes being required, so can the need to change your products or services on offer. You may even have to alter certain aspects of your products or services. Such changes should only happen after much thought has been put into the possible consequences and considering the consistency, practicality, costs, and business quality demand.

Even though your customer may again be unhappy with these changes, they should be aware of the careful consideration you gave before implementing them. Changes are determined by costs, customer feedback, business trends, and the need to provide customers with more value for their money.

Reasons for product or service changes can be:

- either technological in that the equipment or inventory is no longer available or costs too much to keep the price reasonable.
- the cost of having the product or services has increased substantially.
- the customer requests a new product or service for personal or valid reasons.
- hygiene, safety, and security of the customer have compelled you to take steps to limit any injury, loss, or death to them by changing an aspect of your product.

In some cases, a product or service may be changed by removing a particular element. It would help if you replaced it with a suitable alternative.

If the customer has to pay the same price for a product but loses part of it, they may feel exploited and distrust you. The customer will also tell 20 people about the situation, ensuring they'll avoid doing business with you.

All the above-stated sales efforts are those actions you take to promote an increase in sales for your business. In some businesses with limited funds, various methods of developing sales can include internal promotions, external promotions, the use of brochures, synergy with affiliate businesses or experts, and by having a website or commercial page on a social media platform.

For you to research and identify opportunities available, where the minimum cost may be incurred but the most potential sales generated, there may be a few options. You could network with customers, suppliers, and community representatives. And you could scrutinize social media community groups and network with other supporting businesses.

As for trends, they're noticeable habits over time, and there are various ways of establishing your customer's movements. You could interview your customers, staff, or trusted competitors. You could also analyze social media articles and marketing surveys. If you're questioning the stakeholders mentioned above, be aware that their responses are primarily one-sided, subjective, and hugely opinionated.

Instead, ensure you speak to various "respondents" before coming to a concrete conclusion.

Online research, looking at industry analysis, reports, articles, and marketing surveys, will give you a more unbiased and impartial indication of trends. Carefully consider the integrity of the sources or publications you peruse.

Sales Techniques

You use a sales technique or selling method to generate revenue and help you sell better. It isn't all-encompassing and is often learned through trial and error.

The terms "sales process" and "sales method" are sometimes confused as being the same. A sales process covers all the steps you take from a potential customer to an actual one. It's all about opportunities, deals, and your success rate. A sales method (technique) is applied in most processes but often covers only a piece of a process. Instead of outlining steps, it's about skills, focus, and communication. A sales process gets you from point A to point B, whereas a sales technique is the thinking you apply to improve your sales process.

Many sales techniques help you sell better, but you don't necessarily have to choose. You can experiment with some of them or even apply multiple methods to different parts of your sales process.

SPIN Method

SPIN selling (Rackham, 1988) is about you asking the right questions. The wrong questions can bring your sales process to a complete halt. With SPIN, you let your customer do the talking. So what does SPIN stand for? It's an acronym for four sales questions designed to pique the customer's interest and push them to pay you. The acronym is made up of four components, as highlighted below.

- Situation questions will lay the foundation of a sales cycle. Your goal is to understand the potential customer and their situation and check whether your offering can serve their needs. The more you know what to ask, the more valuable the information you'll gather.
- Problem questions will help your potential customer become aware of a problem they need to solve and identify issues they may have overlooked. Where you can show how your products or services can solve a potential customer's problems is where you'll make the sale.
- Implication questions focus on the negative issues a customer may face and where you highlight the urgency for them to use your product or service to resolve it. For example, "If you don't upgrade your operating system now, you could be attacked by hackers or computer viruses."

- Need-Payoff questions arise when a potential customer realizes how their situation or problem might worsen. These questions help them grasp the value of a real solution. Your secret to success is to help your potential customer specify the benefits themselves. If you get these questions right, your potential customer will actually tell you how you can help them.

If you use SPIN as a sales tactic and ask the right questions, you should be successful in making a sale.

SNAP Method

These days, before potential customers can decide what to pay for, they're inundated with information telling them what's better. Because of the latter, getting potential customers' attention has become more challenging. Especially since salespeople are viewed with suspicion, mainly due to many people having been duped or misled into buying or paying for things they didn't need. Laws have become stricter to protect customers, but you should continue selling your offerings.

SNAP selling (Konrath, 2012) allows you to focus on how customers make decisions by influencing them positively. The customer should feel they made the decision on their own.

In essence, customers make various decisions before they decide to hear you out.

- Will they allow you access to them? Customers are inundated with interruptions and distractions and may think your request to see or speak to them wastes time. You must relate relevant information when connecting with them to access their time. Whether by mobile, messenger app, email, etc.
- Are you annoying them? Stop sending generic follow-up messages or emails. Instead, send an email with valuable resources to educate and influence your potential customer. To respect their time, only ask for five-minute meetings or interactions and stick to it. If your potential customer wants to extend the time, leave it up to them. The less time you ask for, the more likely they'll want to chat.
- Why would a potential customer want your product or service? Once a potential customer allows you access to them, you need to quickly demonstrate the value you're offering them and what they can expect to pay you. Share resourceful and bite-sized information that shows how you can meet their needs. Also, keep your ears open for negative words such as "dissatisfaction, challenges, issues, frustration, trouble, and concerns." It will allow you to immerse yourself in helping them solve their problems and have them engage in what you have to offer.

- Are you addressing any limitations or risks your potential customer may face in choosing your product or service? The potential customer is ready to make a decision. Still, they're looking for reasons to justify their choice and minimize risk. A big mistake someone selling makes is to appear too friendly. Instead, focus on helping your potential customer make a decision. You can do this by being flexible and willing to collaborate while clearly stating what they can or can't expect from you. If a potential customer wants something you can't offer, walk away. But if you have something different to offer, highlight it to them.

Consider the following four concepts as you participate in your potential customers' decisions.

- Respect your potential customer's time and make it easy to adopt what you're selling. Have your information ready in bite-sized pieces.
- Rapidly build trust and highlight the value of what you're offering. Show that you genuinely understand your potential customer's business, objectives, or priorities. That will set you apart from most competitors.
- Align with your potential customers' needs, issues, and goals. Have them want to work with you, and you'll quickly gain access to the right decision-makers.

- Focus on priorities. A potential customer will have specific priorities. Selling means understanding those priorities and using them to your advantage. Try and combine their priorities you're your communication. For example, if cost savings are a priority, emphasize that aspect throughout your sales process.

SNAP selling will assist you with knowing what a potential customer thinks. Effectively responding to their thoughts, priorities, and objectives will allow you to win their trust and show them your value.

Challenger Method

This technique developed by Dixon and Anderson (2011) differs from those that focus on a good sales approach being dependent on building relationships with potential customers. It does so because customers are too busy, well-informed, and have many options to invest in a relationship. If you utilize this sales method, you're essentially doing what follows.

- You bring to well-informed potential customers unique information or a new approach to resolving their problems. You educate your potential customers on how they can overcome their challenges differently and uncover needs they don't yet know they have. You're basically providing innovative thinking and guidance while selling them your product or service.

- You tailor-make your communication with each potential customer. The latter is personalized while you remain attuned to their objectives, motivations, needs, and concerns. It's about you adapting to their unique culture and goals.
- You focus on the professional and seek to work with the decision-makers if dealing with a business. To ultimately close a deal, you pursue your goal in a direct, yet nonaggressive, way. If a potential customer resists, you shift the conversation from price to value and challenge their way of thinking.

Below are some tips to put this into action.

- Create a plan for each conversation. Include the desired end goal and have notes on how to get there.
- Ensure there's a two-way exchange of information and value.
- The transaction must be mutually beneficial to you and the potential customer. If it isn't, then walk away.

You'll find that lots of people retain a particular way of thinking. By being assertive but nonaggressive, you can challenge that.

Sandler Method

Applying the Sandler method (Sandler, 1967) is where you act as a reliable and trustworthy source. Strange as it seems, your potential customer is expected to convince you to sell to them with this method. To achieve the latter, you have deep and heartfelt discussions with your potential customer, moving beyond technical aspects and focusing on the impact a challenge or issue has on them. Besides what your possible customer experiences on the technical side of a need or problem, they highlight their priority needs. To get a potential customer to this point, focus on the three following areas.

- Explores the technical aspects of the potential customer's issue while encouraging them to look at the issue problem on a business and personal level. This way, they will convince you that they need to spend money on what you're offering. You'll focus on their needs from the first meeting while avoiding any demonstration or presentation of your offer.
- Usually, a potential customer isn't convinced to pay for something because it will help them solve a technical issue or need. Regardless, your solution will bring them value, such as saving them time and money, which they can spend on other relevant projects. In that case, it's where you'll get their attention.

Go beyond using cost-saving reasoning. Instead, spell out your solution's impact on them or their business. For example, allowing them to focus on other, possibly more important, priorities.

- Attempt to put a potential customer's issues in a personal context. People often make decisions for personal reasons and not only for practical or financial reasons. A potential customer who can personally gain something from your solution will be more committed to what you're offering. It could save them from working overtime or spending too much effort on a task or activity. Getting to this point depends on whether your potential customer convinces you, and more importantly themselves, that a solution is a very high personal priority.

Identifying the above is integral to moving beyond a technical attribute or issue by magnifying the importance of acting with a sense of urgency. In other words, this technique has you focus on the financial and personal impact your product or service will have on your potential customer. In addition to using the technical aspects to support the solution you propose.

Consultative Method

With this solutions selling technique (Hanan, 1970), you act as an expert consultant and ask questions to determine your potential customer's needs.

Your focus is on how they feel when they're talking to you. Then your goal is to form a long-term connection with them by putting them first. This consultative selling method focuses on six principles.

- First, do your research by gathering all the information you can get about your potential customer before meeting with them. Look for information about your competitors to see how you rank up against them. The aim is for you to become an expert before you connect with your potential customer. You can also ensure you anticipate any questions they may have so you're well prepared.
- Ask your potential customer the right questions about their needs and challenges. Begin with general questions and move on to more specific ones. It will assist you in understanding the context, allowing you to build an idea of how your solution is better suited to the potential customer.
- Be genuinely interested in your prospect. Listen and absorb as much information as possible. Note what's said and, more importantly, what's not said. Nonverbal cues, such as their tone of voice, are just as important as what they tell you. Let your potential customer do most of the talking and only ask clarifying questions. Then, when done, summarize your main takeaways to avoid misunderstanding.

Keep your eyes and ears open for what they find important to them or their business if they have one.

- Instead of teaching your potential customer about your product or service, help them overcome a challenge or meet a need. Help them build a plan to reach their goals, and ensure your "why" is evident throughout your conversations. It would help if you emphasized that you're there to help them advance or improve.
- If you have a chance to assist a potential customer, dedicate your time and attention. Then, follow through but don't come across as too insistent on closing a deal. You want to stay at the forefront of their minds without being seen as annoying or pushy. If you've listened well and taken notes, you can use the information to send them the relevant information should you not have heard from them in a while.
- Closing the deal should be easy for those potential customers you've qualified as high-potential and thus invested your efforts and resources in getting the sale. Suppose the potential customer pushes back toward not going ahead with the sale. In that case, you can drive their focus to see the consequences if they decide to leave their situation or issue as is.

A sale achieved using this technique should result in one of the following three things.

- A customer achieves their goal.
- You solve a customer's problem.
- You satisfy a customer's need.

Solution selling is aimed at building long-term relationships between you and your customers. You're helping your customers succeed throughout the entire selling process. And the only natural way to do so is to listen to them.

Summary

The techniques discussed in this chapter all emphasize the importance of qualifying potential customers. Only sell to some people you encounter, but talk to potential customers to ascertain if you can offer them what they really need.

- SPIN will have you ask the right questions of your potential customers to uncover their needs.
- SNAP will help you focus on the way your potential customers think and how you can react to that.
- The Challenger tactic will have you focus on a potential customer's specific way of thinking to challenge and create a new perspective.
- The Sandler technique will have you showing your potential customers the technical, financial, and personal impact their choices may have on them.

- The Consultative selling method will have you invest in long-term relationships with your chosen potential customers. It won't be about asking or showing them things anymore but about listening to them instead.

Selling effectively and closing a deal faster is applying the correct sales method that works for you. But remember, you can only sell what you believe in.

CHAPTER 4: QUALITY IS EVERYTHING

Since customers are spoilt for choice these days, you wonder whether quality still matters. Yes, it does. It isn't just about offering a product or service made to a standard but also about the reputation you gain for consistently providing exceptional products or services. For any business, big or small, quality is crucial.

Definition

The word "quality" comes from the Latin word *qualis*, which means "of what kind" or "of such a kind." In other words, it's not just about what you produce or serve but how you present or do it.

Thus, quality should be maintained in all aspects for your business to succeed. Every product, service, process, task, action, or decision you make can be judged by how it's executed. Managing quality affects how your business performs. It can also differentiate you from your competitors, thus attracting potential customers.

Delivering quality products or services comes down to three things.

1. You have a robust system of procedures, verifications, and checks based on your objectives and how to achieve them.
2. You ensure you have assurance measures to check and re-check that how things are done matches what you expect.
3. You continuously strive to do things better.

To maintain quality, you can develop procedures to ensure the way you prefer to do things is done by anyone working for or with you in your business. Your main aim should be to enhance customer satisfaction and drive your business's growth.

Importance

Quality's essential because it allows you to keep up with or even exceed what your competitors are doing. Your products or services have to be seen by customers as superior. Having the correct procedures and checks to see if the former is correctly executed helps you achieve cost efficiency and the proper utilization of resources available.

Good quality management can enhance your brand and reputation. It can protect you from risk, increase your business's efficiency, boost profits, and reduce waste.

All of these allow your business to grow while creating customer satisfaction.

Profitability

There's a correlation between your quality levels and profitability. Though it requires more investment from you, in the form of money and effort, it definitely has a return on investment. Fewer failures or defects lead to less money wasted or opportunities lost. Conversely, any improvements in performance, features, or other dimensions of your products or services, will lead to increased sales and a larger market share.

Efficiency

Quality management will help you improve your products' reliability, durability, and performance. If you don't sell products but only services, your quality management will build loyalty, trust, and, again, business performance. Better products or services equal happier customers and more sales.

Remember, though, that once a customer buys a product or pays for a service from you, they'll expect the same quality every time. Suppose you don't have a quality management system. In that case, your customers will find differences in what they pay for, every time they return to you. The latter can irritate and, as a consequence, alienate them.

Having verification checks in place to check products before selling them or reviewing service level agreements as you provide a service will ensure you maintain a high standard.

The way you can implement a quality management system that will create an environment that's efficient and supports a quality culture requires you to follow specific steps.

1. Clarify your vision, mission, and values. It clarifies where you're headed and ties in with your strategy. If you have staff, they should understand where you're heading (your vision), what you want to accomplish (your mission), and the principles you work by (your values). All of these influence how you make decisions.

2. Identify your business's critical success factors. These help you focus on those things that help you meet your objectives and thus move you toward achieving your mission. Turning these factors into performance-based measures will help you ascertain how well your business is doing. For example, these factors can include financial performance, customer reviews, process improvement, size of your market share, and product quality test results.

3. Develop measures to track your critical success factors data. Once you've identified your factors, you need to measure them to monitor and track your progress. It can be done through a reporting process.

For example, your goal is to increase customer satisfaction survey scores. In that case, you should state a goal and a measure to demonstrate that you're achieving that goal.

4. Identify your key customer groups. You should know your key customer groups because you create your products or services based on their requirements. The mistake a lot of businesses make is to not acknowledge their staff as a key customer group. Some other key customer groups you have are your customers, suppliers, service providers, vendors, and volunteers or interns. Please get to know each customer group by identifying what their needs are.

5. Ask for customer feedback. You'll only know how well you're meeting your customers' requirements by asking them. Create a process to ask for input from each customer group to identify what's important to them and how they're experiencing your offering. Please don't assume you think you know what's important to your customers and ask them the wrong questions. Instead, remember that what your customer expects today differs from what they expected a year ago. Likewise, what your customer expects today will vary from what they expect a year from now.

6. Develop a survey tool. You create a customer satisfaction survey tool based on what's important to your customers.

For example, your customers might care more about quality than price. So, suppose you're developing a product and trying to keep the costs down by sacrificing quality. In that case, you're not meeting your customers' expectations. It would help if you learned to balance the cost of creating your products or providing your services and your customers' perceived value. Survey each customer group by creating a customized survey for each of them. It'll help you establish a baseline for their perception of your current practices and processes.

7. Develop an improvement plan for your business. Once you have the baseline established for what your different customer groups require, you can set up an improvement plan. Ensure your improvement plan is specific, measurable, achievable, realistic, and linked to a time frame (Doran, Miller, and Cunningham, 1981).

8. Resurvey to see if what you're doing is actually working. After implementing your improvement plan, take some time and do another survey to see if your results have changed. Remember that your customer groups' needs may vary, so be attuned to those changes.

9. Incorporate your customer satisfaction data into your marketing efforts. Once you've achieved some positive results, show them to your potential customers.

Customers want to know your business processes work, primarily if the latter benefits them.
10. Maintain current technology because that's how work gets done. Use technology to your advantage and commit to keeping up with changes. Just ensure the technology is easy to use. For example, your website or social media page should be easy to use and locate and have easy-to-understand content.

Whatever internal processes and measures you put in place, if you have staff, ensure they understand your vision and the role they play in it. Successful quality initiatives require your ongoing leadership and support.

Satisfaction

These days, customers are more demanding than ever. They can choose from and have access to a vast number of brands. If your products or services fail to meet your customers' expectations, your brand and sales will suffer.

Customers want their money spent on things that are worth the price they're charged. You lose them forever if something is of poor quality or even defective. A proper quality management system or process can help you turn potential customers into paying ones. You'll achieve this by continuously improving your products, incorporating changes, double-checking every process, and eliminating defects or service lapses.

If you want your business to stand out, it's critical to meet or exceed your customers' expectations.

Customer satisfaction leads to customer loyalty. So, if customers are satisfied with your product or service, they'll return. However, if you deliver a defective product or incompetent service, they'll be more likely to never return.

Protection

When it comes to products, once they leave your premises, there are still risks to consider. Recalls, for instance, can result in financial losses and affect your customers' experiences. If they impact your customers' health or property negatively, you can stand to lose even more. It will also most likely damage your brand and reputation.

It's incredible how one defective or harmful product can impact your business. If a customer buys a defective product from you that hasn't been checked, they'll ask for a refund and return the item. Then, to make matters worse, they'll probably not buy from you again and tell a few of their friends and colleagues about it. Worse still is if they leave a poor review online, thus warning other people not to buy from you.

You have different risks to consider if you don't sell products but provide services or expertise.

Not delivering what you promised or causing your customers financial or physical harm will make you liable for the losses associated with your negligence. As with defective products, you'll also damage your brand and reputation.

It only takes one disgruntled customer to tell a few friends and colleagues about your poor service delivery. The damage to your brand will be further compounded if they leave a bad review online, thus cautioning others not to use your services.

As a business owner, you're responsible for bearing the costs of product recalls and poor service delivery. If your failure impacted customers substantially, financially, or physically, you could also face legal consequences. So, pay attention to the importance of quality management.

Cost Savings

The better your quality management system and the better you display your quality when delivering your offering, the more customers you'll get and the more you'll earn. It's due to you building a good reputation from having great products or exceptional services. Customers will recommend your business to their friends and colleagues and return to you, thus creating repeat business.

Quality improvement can be made in various areas of your business, such as:

- marketing and sales
- administration
- finance and accounting
- research
- manufacturing
- equipment maintenance
- recruitment
- customer service

When applied consistently over time, the above processes can reduce costs and increase profit. For example, a quality product or service requires less rework, leading to cost savings and fewer claims against you.

Meeting Standards

Adherence to a recognized quality standard for the industry in which you operate is essential for dealing with specific customers or complying with applicable laws. Some businesses may insist that their suppliers, you, in this case, achieve accreditation with quality standards. Suppose you're in the healthcare, food, or electrical goods industries. In that case, you must comply with health and safety standards designed to protect customers.

If you aren't required to do so but want to set up the required quality control steps in your business, look online for standards about your industry. You can then incorporate what is valuable and practical into your business processes. Some companies specialize in assisting businesses with setting up a quality management system and measuring compliance. The latter may prove expensive for a small business, though.

Accredited quality control systems will ensure you comply with those standards. But accreditation can also help you attract new customers or enter new markets by confirming that you provide quality products or services to potential customers.

Waste Reduction

If you're fortunate to find a product that's unsuitable for selling, you'll have to dispose of it, thus costing you money. It's lucky because you discovered it and not your customer. The same applies if you realize your business has wasted hours on a job for a customer. If you find many items that need to be put up to standard or hours destroyed, your business will generate a lot of waste and time wasted over a year.

Motivating

Interestingly, the better your quality management, the happier you and your staff are. We're all motivated when we don't have to constantly deal with unhappy customers or faulty products. Spending time resolving problems that could've been prevented is demoralizing. It takes us away from growing the business and improving our reputation.

Your staff will be motivated to keep your standards if they know that each product is made correctly and checked before it's sold. Though it may seem laborious, guidelines for producing goods or doing work helps eliminate guesswork and ensures compliance. Rather than becoming complacent after a while, you and your staff can work smarter to guarantee everything you offer will meet or exceed your customers' expectations.

CHAPTER 5: WHAT IS CONSISTENCY?

Being consistent is far more critical than you realize. It allows you to establish awareness, build trust and deliver your products or services efficiently. Without it, your business will most likely make no or a limited profit. It could even fail.

Consistency is a fundamental requirement if your aim is to establish trust with your customers. You're asking potential customers to buy from you because you'll deliver what you say you'll provide. You're stating that your product or service will be on time, at the agreed price, and be of superior quality. And, when you're selling your product or service, you're making these promises. Unfortunately, it's no different than what your competitors are doing, so what can you do to stand out?

Simply telling everyone that you're reliable and trustworthy is just using your words. It means nothing until you prove it. Once you get an order, you're positioned to make an impression. But what about before you get an order? How will you make your potential customer feel comfortable with what you're promising them?

One way to do so is to show your performance statistics. If you can show your good online ratings or how you've had a great delivery score from your customers for the last year, it will go a long way to appease their fears.

If you're able to do so, all the better. Interestingly, having online testimonials on rating platforms or social media pages will help you. It's because these comments or testimonials focus on overall satisfaction and quality. One way to ensure you have more positive ratings and accompanying testimonials is to encourage every one of your customers to do so.

Another way to prove your consistency is to control your customers' expectations. Always under-promise and over-deliver. If you promise the stars to get you the deal, the risk is that you may disappoint to some degree. Instead, promise within your range of possibilities but then deliver exceptionally well. You can expand the conversation to include other services or products. Patience and attention to detail are the main requirements for success.

Be cautious when applauding your consistency in casual conversation. If you, for example, tell a potential customer that your favorite football team is A. Still, next year you tell them you're supporting team B. You could be showing yourself as inconsistent. Your customer may then view your business the same. You may think you're being adaptive or flexible, but in reality, you appear unreliable. And reliability is more valued in business than flexibility. If you can change so quickly, you could appear opportunistic and inconsistent.

Also, if you tell a customer one thing and later contradict yourself, trust between you two is destroyed. And trust, once broken, is nearly impossible to get back. For various reasons, your ability to deliver the same product or service at the agreed level is only sometimes possible. Your customer might understand if you have a reasonable and plausible explanation for why the variation happened and that it won't happen again. We all know that things sometimes go wrong, despite our best efforts. But it's how we deal with it that customers look at. What follows is some advice on how you could perform more consistently.

Align Your Efforts

You must realize early on that every decision and action you take must contribute to accomplishing the purpose of your business and its existence. Every business operates like a clock. Whether it works efficiently or not depends on the stability and smooth function of every one of its parts.

Define Your Brand

You're expected to get bored using the same brand elements every day. But consistency is critical regarding your visual brand and how you represent it. Changing colors, images, features, and fonts can make your brand appear unprofessional.

A solid brand differentiates your business from your competitors. However, if you don't consistently live up to your brand's promises, your ability to retain customers will reduce. If you look at the actions of powerful brands, you'll note how they're consistent in strategy, implementation, and representation. Any changes they make are few and far between.

Keep Your Plans

Any leader or manager must commit to following a specific action plan. This is the same for a business owner, freelancer, or entrepreneur. If you don't, you can put yourself in danger of generating high amounts of debt or even going out of business.

Every time you choose to change your plans too early, you risk increasing costs without receiving any benefits from what you originally planned. You can ill afford to make terrible financial decisions based on inconsistent actions. You could lose your business in this way.

Review Your Results

Remember that it often takes time to see the results of your efforts. You receive wavering results if your business processes, sales, and marketing efforts are inconsistent.

For example, running a booster campaign for a day or two will give you little if no insight into how successful your advertisement is. If you instead do the campaign for a set period, you can receive better insight into how the campaign is working for you. Ending the campaign too early may sabotage what you're trying to achieve.

Moving Forward

Though consistency in how you interact with your customers allows you to build a loyal customer base, it also provides them with exceptional experiences. It's essential to understand your customers' needs and wants while meeting their expectations every time. Whether establishing your brand or planning your sales strategy, you must recognize the power of consistency. You can gain an advantage over your competitors by becoming consistent in all your endeavors.

CHAPTER 6: IT TAKES A VILLAGE

To emphasize the value a community plays on your business, let's briefly look at the psychological and practical implications the concept of community has on all of us.

Relationships are essential to us all. We often link our health, contentment, and a sense of purpose to the relationships we value. As human beings, we're relational by nature. If we're isolated or detached from a community, we immediately see our physical and mental health compromised.

Whatever we endeavor to create or achieve is subject to the social connections we have. These interactions can shape our brains' physical structure and development, leading to integrated or disintegrated mental states.

When we cultivate a community for ourselves, we can do the following.

- We must be intentional about creating and maintaining one. It requires us to go out and meet people. Start new conversations, join groups, or reconnect with old acquaintances. Our community doesn't have physical limits, especially these days. Thanks to smartphones, social media, and messaging apps, distance doesn't need to separate us.

- The quality of our relationships often depends on how vulnerable we are with others and the degree to which we respect others' vulnerabilities. How we feel in times of uncertainty, risk, or emotional exposure and how we relate our situations with others form the foundation of authentic relationships. The latter often requires these emotional risks. So, if we want to experience deeper relationships and, subsequently, a shared connection with others, we have to be willing to share our struggles and successes with those we come to know and trust. Our vulnerability presents itself when we let our authentic selves be seen and understood by others. It's ironically an antidote to shame and a foundation for building trust and connection.

When we build a community, it doesn't mean we have to befriend every new person we meet. Likewise, we don't have to go out every weekend to socialize. A sense of community can be nurtured by taking small steps, such as starting a conversation with your neighbor. Thus, building a community for yourself begins with small, intentional acts of kindness and acknowledgments.

Importance

A community provides you with many elements, but three of those are most beneficial.

- If you've ever felt like you didn't belong, you know it can be an isolating experience. Being part of a community provides you with a sense of belonging. It isn't about conforming but feeling part of a community as your authentic self. You're not required to change who you are to be a part thereof. Still, you're accepted and appreciated for your unique qualities and contributions.
- Having people you can call upon when you need to talk or need assistance helps you through difficult situations. Knowing some people who support you can help you feel secure, emotionally and physically, thus benefiting your outlook on life.
- Being part of a community means everyone has a different role. You may be the friend who's an expert in the kitchen and can be counted on to bring a comforting meal over when someone is going through a difficult time. Or you're the friend others know they can call upon when they need to discuss challenges they're experiencing. It makes you an active member of your community and provides you with a purpose.

Having a purpose, and helping others, gives life meaning, but most of all, it provides you with a network that can help your business grow.

It would help to start with self-reflection when looking for a strong sense of connection. Knowing what's important to you can help you connect with others who think and feel the same. You may enjoy golf and could join a golf club. Or you've always wanted to try archery, and you just heard there's an archery club in town. It can be anything that makes connecting with others easier while doing the activities you enjoy.

You can also ask yourself what your values are. These values could lead you to connect with local charities, volunteer work, or even religious activities. Being of service is rewarding and has the added benefit of allowing you to connect with others with similar values. Remember, a significant part of building a community is giving back to one another. Finding volunteer or charity work is a great way to start.

If you connect with a spiritual or religious belief, try attending speaking engagements, introductory classes, or religious services. A political cause may speak to you. If so, join a group that works towards a meaningful goal for you. Connecting with something bigger than yourself is another valuable way to broaden your community.

Where you find your community is up to you. If you have yet to find a strong sense of community up until now, keep trying.

Whether your community is big or small, finding people you can connect with is vital for your mindset and future success. And remember, just as you need to find your community, it's also essential for others to have you as part of their community.

Development

Businesses involved in their communities gain benefits that positively affect their profit margins. They notice an increase in customer retention as well as more engaged staff. If you're deliberate about making a positive impact in your community, it will positively affect your business.

Building relationships with people within your community is a great promotional tool. The relationships help you keep your business message relevant. It also enables you to imprint a positive image of your brand. The members of your community develop a positive image of your business since they know you'll listen to their concerns.

If you have staff, they can act as your ambassadors by engaging in community events and addressing community needs. If they're volunteering, it offers them opportunities to practice leadership and other life skills. They'll interact with a diverse group of people and become accustomed to the various talents and ways people do things. In addition, they may perform multiple leadership roles, which will garner vital experience.

The range of skill building is limitless, and with each new volunteering opportunity comes a different situation with a different set of circumstances, each handled in a new and different way. All to the benefit of your business in the end.

You can also increase morale by having you and your team focus on community involvement. People appreciate being part of a successful and winning team. There's pride in knowing we're participating in something larger than ourselves.

Community involvement offers you and your staff both personal satisfaction and personal development. They'll be more willing to outperform when they know their efforts are making more of a difference than simply making your business money. Intelligent leaders always emphasize the connection between the values of a business, its staff, and its community.

Involvement

In what ways are you and your business involved in your community? How are you helping staff grow and develop through volunteer projects if you have a team? If you aren't interested, now's the time to find ways to contribute to your community's success.

Working for yourself can be extremely rewarding but also challenging. Isolation isn't just useless and leaves you feeling alone; it also poses a genuine risk to your health. When no one's around, you must navigate the challenges of owning a business yourself. You need more support to thrive as an entrepreneur.

It's here where your business community comes in. Fostering a solid professional network can give you the means to confidently face business challenges. What follows is how you can integrate into your business community.

Collaboration

Can you recall a moment in your past when you received feedback about something you were working on? Didn't your project suddenly feel more impactful or exciting? Whenever you're having difficulty finding the right words or can't put your finger on what's missing, having a fresh set of eyes is almost always bound to improve. Thus, collaboration brings out our best work. Unfortunately, as an entrepreneur or freelancer, it's only sometimes possible.

One of the most challenging elements of going into business alone is that you'll often face decisions alone. You won't have a sounding board to bounce ideas off of or to give you advice. Even if your family is involved, they can't be relied upon to be impartial or objective. You may lack access to a trusted expert to give you professional advice.

Many online or physical communities allow you to ask them for advice. It can help you find the words to deal with a rude customer or proofread your advertisement before submitting it for publication. Besides, growth never happens in a vacuum.

When you're a part of a community, you can find business allies and grow your customer base. Take heed, though. You don't want to enter a community to only see what you can take or get. You do so to also take part in giving back. I recall managing a small hotel located in a suburb over a decade ago. I did get customers from the community I was based in. Still, I also made a point of supporting the businesses inside that community, where plausible, thus avoiding traveling elsewhere to spend my money. My hotel and I had both our reputations spread positively and beneficially. As a result, even though most of my customers were from out of town, they were referred by local businesses and people to my hotel. Even though there were over ten other hotels close by.

Accountability

There's a reason clubs and online communities exist. Holding others accountable, and you being held responsible by others, is more straightforward than holding yourself accountable.

As an entrepreneur or freelancer, you have to have self-discipline and self-reliance.

However, having a group of peers rally behind you and check in on your progress is excellent motivation and builds your business simultaneously. So, being part of a business community is about sharing goals and returning to them frequently. You use others to hold you accountable for your performance while doing the same for them. The point is to get the job done.

Respite

Unfortunately, things happen. When they do, you want a safe place to go to. Whether you're doubtful about a potential customer or concerned about a problem, your community is the perfect place to connect with and get valuable feedback. They most likely have faced the same situation as you on a prior occasion.

Your community, personal or business, is the perfect place to share your frustrations or validate any concerns you may have. On the flip side, it's also the ideal environment to return to and celebrate any wins you achieve.

Finding a Community

The first step in finding a community you can be part of, whether on a one-to-one basis or as a business, is to show up. It will depend on your business, but ideally, you'll want to find diverse groups with whom you share an affinity.

It could be the type of products or services you provide or your personal interests. An excellent place to begin is to search for social media groups in your niche or check with your peers if they have any recommendations. Alternatively, contact your local Chamber of Commerce if you want to meet local business owners.

Then, consider attending networking events. Sure, they can be creepy because they attract all sorts of people. But they don't have to be. Other small businesses in your area may host these events with a more professional approach. Regardless, if there aren't any networking events in your area, how about hosting your own? Sometimes when you're looking for someone to follow or emulate, you realize you're the person best suited to fulfill that role. It can be scary, but courage never exists in the absence of fear. And to be afraid is a choice.

If you're working from home, you'll only meet people if you venture outside. Put yourself out there. Try renting a booth at a market or head to your local coffee shop. Don't be afraid to strike up a conversation. It allows you to connect with other entrepreneurs or creative people in an environment that doesn't feel staged or forced. You may stumble upon a new customer while doing so. Starting and running a business is hard enough as it is. You don't need to make it harder by doing it yourself. The people you surround yourself with can impact how you experience entrepreneurship. It takes a village for you to succeed. You can't do so by yourself.

CHAPTER 7: WORD-OF-MOUTH

Now we get to the most potent form of marketing, namely word-of-mouth marketing. It's when a customer's interest in your products or services is reflected in their daily conversations with others. It's free advertising triggered by your customer's great experiences with you, your products, or your services.

I recall working for an international hotel group that developed a novel budget hotel concept in the 1980s. They were easy to build and offered people only what they needed: a clean room, a bed, a wash area, air-conditioning, a television, and a quick breakfast in the morning. The hotels were well-located near main travel hubs such as airports. You could even check yourself in using an automated machine that gave you a code to access the hotel and your room.

Where word-of-mouth marketing comes in is that after their launch, they didn't do any marketing except rely on their customers talking about their convenience and affordable rates. What started as a few hotels went on to them having over 1,500 in Europe, Africa, Asia, and South America by the late 1990s. These budget hotels even contributed over 80% of their entire group's cash. Considering the group also had over 2,500 other hotels ranging from 2- to 5-star hotels, the budget hotel's cash contribution was nothing to sneeze at. All of their success was based on word-of-mouth marketing.

Customer-to-customer communications can attract potential customers, which is why online reviews are so powerful these days. Word-of-mouth marketing is also facilitated by social media posts. The latter can contain customers sharing their experiences with your business visually or making statements that show a positive emotional connection between what they needed and what you delivered.

Definition

Word-of-mouth marketing occurs when customers talk about your business's products or services with friends, colleagues, staff, family, and other people they're close to.

It's the most powerful form of advertising since customers trust their friends' recommendations over what the media tells them. Whether the media is traditional or contemporary.

You can encourage this form of marketing by exceeding your customers' expectations of what you provide, how well you treat them and giving them complete information. It's about being honest, credible, social, measurable, consistent, and respectful.

You can rely on something other than a customer for word-of-mouth marketing, as there are different ways to attempt to drive word-of-mouth references to your business. When you notice a customer make a positive comment online, share it with your followers on social media.

You can do the same if you're part of a community group on social media. Just don't overdo it because you may come across as insincere.

You could also encourage your customers to "spread the word," so to speak. And you can do so by giving them a reason to do so, such as exceeding their expectations or providing insider skills about a product. You could also add surprise moments that benefit them beyond what they expect.

Other strategies include offering customers new ways to share information about your products or services and engaging with them through exemplary customer service. This is especially valuable with social media-based customer service, which provides you with an opportunity for effortless sharing. The latter then promotes your business.

Most people trust recommendations from friends, family, and colleagues above all other forms of advertising. It shows you just how effective word-of-mouth marketing can be. And customers are emotionally bonded to your business if they believe you listen to them. It's why many businesses will have sales representatives discuss their products and services with customers one-on-one. These interactions, as well as promotional events, can encourage conversations about your products or services.

For example, let's say you make and sell a fantastic sauce. You could have a special promotion where a chef (or you're playing the role) teaches potential customers how to make dishes or BBQ meat with your sauce as a distinctive feature. Ensure you have enough inventory on hand should people go nuts after tasting your creation. Most people buy on impulse when they've just enjoyed or participated in something. Also, ensure the recipes you use are printed onto little cards for you to hand out. Then your customers can try and replicate what you made at home, using your sauce of course. Don't give them your sauce recipe though.

Refrain from faking word-of-mouth marketing because it can backfire on you. In many countries, advertising codes of ethics ensure that businesses' marketing strategies are credible, responsible, and respectful but never misleading or dishonest. Instead, you can have a loyalty program, which will reward customers for their repeated business. These loyalty programs can provide your customers with the means to provide feedback and partake in any giveaways or competitions you run.

When looking at the digital version of word-of-mouth marketing, you use technology, particularly the internet, to facilitate word-of-mouth exchanges. Review sites, social media pages, and blogs are popular platforms your customers can use to share their good or bad experiences. Shared testimonials will significantly influence your potential and current customers' buying decisions.

But when you respond to positive and negative reviews online, be honest, appreciative, and genuine. More people will want to share their experiences when they notice you do so and that you do it respectfully and professionally.

Importance

Word-of-mouth marketing is crucial since it's an effective way to increase sales. It promotes your products or services, increases your brand's recognition, and builds customer loyalty. Many businesses utilize strategies that prompt customers to recommend their services or products and share positive experiences. You can create the spark that causes conversations among your customers. Since we know most people trust the advice of their family and friends' advice, focusing on word-of-mouth marketing can be very beneficial.

If it still needs to be a strategy you've considered, the time is now. Word-of-mouth marketing is cost-effective, builds brand loyalty, and reveals new ways to reach potential customers. It usually occurs over dinner parties, texts, and casual encounters between friends, colleagues, and family. It can also be through social media or community blogs.

Types

Referrals to your business can come from several sources.

Still, for sales and marketing purposes, the following most essential channels are what you should know about.

- A friend says to a friend, "I was just with the best yoga instructor. She's so professional and helpful. You should join me next time!" The latter is the most basic form of word-of-mouth marketing. When customers get a recommendation from a friend they trust, they're far more likely to look at the product or service recommended to them. You can only measure this type of marketing by asking your new customers how they heard of your offering. If they say, "A friend told me about you," you can ask them what their friend liked. Here, you'll discover what is helping you build your brand in the market.
- Your sales representative sets up a market stall and offers people a sample of your new product. Here face-to-face marketing is usually more business-like. It's a sales process, but it's still a one-on-one tactic. The potential customer also has an opportunity to give you immediate feedback. In addition, your sales representative can tell them more about your brand and hand over a business card or flyer.
- A customer went to your restaurant and was so happy with their experience that they created user-generated content (UGC). They posted a picture of their meal, added a video, and gave your restaurant a 5-star review on social media and a rating page.

Once a UGC is created, you can use the content to show off an unbiased testimonial and to build a strong relationship with the customer who posted their experience. UGC can reach a larger audience than what's intended by the customer. If you can harness UGC, you've found one of the easiest and most cost-effective ways to grow your online presence.

There are elements of social media marketing in the above marketing options. Still, posts on any platform that mention your brand are powerful instances of social proof. Engage when you're tagged. Customers love it when brands respond, so be encouraged to like, share, and comment when you're tagged.

Strategies

Word-of-mouth marketing is a universal concept, which makes it incredibly valuable. Unfortunately, it also makes it difficult to measure and even control.

So, how can you measure your success and implement a strategy to improve your chances for face-to-face recommendations? How can you quickly find and address negative reviews or comments and protect your reputation? Let's look at your options for implementing these tactics into your marketing strategy.

Create Conversations

Your brand gets its best exposure during peer-to-peer conversations. Word-of-mouth marketing is about people sharing their feelings and thoughts about your products or service, thereby indirectly soliciting sales for you. It's a ripple effect.

How can you keep their conversation going? First, find out where conversations are happening. You do so by understanding your audience. Where do they hang out? Online social groups or communities are a great place to start but ensure you adhere to any guidelines. Often advertising isn't allowed so be involved without promoting your products or services. Remember, you're trying to do research. Of course, if you're asked a question about your products or services you're allowed to answer.

You can only market to an audience if you understand who they are. These days it's even more complicated. Customers aren't easily classified into groups or other demographic indications. Look at your own data and see what types of customers you have and what content they respond to. Whether it's online or via prior interactions, you had with them.

Your online reputation is vital. If you notice a lot of negative comments, address them swiftly and professionally. Don't let it fester and get out of control.

You won't just solve the issue quicker, but it will also leave a positive impression on current and potential customers. Having a good "crisis communication strategy" is essential, but it's imperative when you're prioritizing your word-of-mouth marketing efforts. There are alert tools that can help notify you when something has been posted about you or your business online.

Encourage UGC

Generally speaking, user-generated content makes a brand more authentic to people. So how can you encourage people to create content and thereby help you promote your business?

- Create a brand hashtag to invite customers to tag you.
- Take note of trending topics on social media and see how you can apply them to your brand by mentioning and tagging them.
- Run an online competition or incentivize your followers with special discounts or free giveaways.
- Ask for customer feedback to hear what they want.
- Share reviews and stories from your customers.

Customer reviews are a great tactic and should be part of your word-of-mouth marketing strategy. Remember that most customers trust online reviews. It's a significant aspect of online marketing. Thousands of strangers trust what others say about your products or services online.

Any accomplishments or awards your business receives should be shared on your website, social media platforms, advertising campaigns, or third-party sites. They can be written statements, video interviews, or a complete story in an article. Using positive customer stories is also an excellent word-of-mouth marketing practice. But remember, except for a public review site, all other posts or material shared by a customer online needs their permission before you share it yourself.

Brand Ambassadors

If you recall, we looked at influencers earlier on. They are your brand ambassadors with significant followers who promote products and services. In other words, they promote your brand on social and video platforms.

Influencers are powerful because they're trusted by potential customers. But, unlike a one-on-one connection, they're speaking to a much larger audience. And the best part is that it's easier to measure your return on investment if you're working with them officially.

Just be aware that they're often expensive, and the more followers they have, the more it will cost you. Having a significant number of followers is only sometimes the answer. Ask prospective influencers about their engagement metrics to see how active their audience is.

If you're thinking of using an influencer to market your business, consider the following questions:

- do they fit your brand image?
- have they worked with your competitors?
- who is their audience?
- does this make sense for your budget?

You could reach thousands or even millions of people by engaging an influencer. But please take note, ensure you can service them when they come calling, and also be aware that most of the people who follow the influencer you choose can actually afford your products or services. They should also be the type of followers who'd be interested in what you have to offer.

Listening

Look at how people talk about your industry and pay particular attention to their frustrations and challenges. Take a step back and really listen. It will help you direct conversations and apply solutions based on what people are saying. Likewise, you can track the type of content your audience enjoys, such as photos, videos, snap stories, etc. The latter will provide clues to maximize a return on building an engaged following. This following will continue spreading the word to their friends and followers. Though, remember the invaluable information you can gather from tracking your competitors as well.

Just be careful. There are a lot of services out there that promise to track online behavior or provide you with statistics that you may or may not be able to use. Honestly, worry about that when you're no longer a small business. You can spend thousands on something you may need more time to prepare for. In management, we call that economies of scale. In other words, it's whether the size of your business and what it produces, distributes, or serves is enough that you can suddenly increase output to meet a surge in demand.

Benefit Your Business

So, let's review the main benefits of using word-of-mouth marketing.

- It's low cost because you aren't paying it if it's true. It impacts your sales with little to no advertising spend.
- It builds trust, reputation, and customer loyalty. Developing confidence in your business takes time and effort. Since recommendations come from friends, the customer trusts them. In addition, online reviews are inherently trustworthy, especially when compared to simply telling everyone how great you are.

- It creates long-term value. Gaining consistent, cheerful chatter around your products or services through word-of-mouth marketing will help you keep repeat customers and make it easier to engage influencers for partnerships.

A customer referred by people they know and trust is more loyal to a brand, on average, than those who stumbled upon your business by chance.

CHAPTER 8: HAVE SOME STANDARDS

As an entrepreneur, freelancer, or small business, you already know that you must work twice as hard to prove yourself against larger enterprises. It's here where standards come in. Whether you want to improve quality, implement a customer management system, or build credibility with your customers, using standards can help.

By implementing standards, you inspire confidence in your business, and it sets you apart from your competition. It can also save money, boost productivity, and improve profitability. Having standards in place can do the following for you.

- It can help you allocate resources efficiently.
- It can quickly get your product to market.
- It can reduce the risks of failure.
- It can help you compete with other businesses.

It can also help you retain existing customers and open doors to new customers and markets. Indeed, some larger customers, such as businesses, require you to have standards in place.

Definition

Standards define how your company operates, thus creating trust in your brand. Guidelines can describe quality, performance, safety, risk aversion methods, production metrics, etc. Your standards can comply with the law or professional organizations such as is required for medical practitioners or financial advisors. Or, you could institute them to create confidence in your customers. For example, if you run a restaurant, your standard is to only use locally-sourced ingredients.

Whatever standards you implement must align with your mission and objectives and apply consistently. If you have staff, they need to adhere to your standards. Everyone is working toward the same goal and honoring your business's promise to the customer.

Purpose

Personally, you have your own set of values, beliefs, and performance standards. Likewise, your business needs these characteristics, which form part of your business standards. As such, your business standards will likely reflect your personal standards. Your customers and staff will form an opinion about your business and brand based on them.

Standards can be split into sections to include how the customer is treated, what is offered, what the products or services are, and how your business is maintained. Other areas can include how sales are captured and filed, reports are generated, expense payments are completed, banking is handled, and what to do in case of a refund. Then you may have a section on how computer information is controlled, fires prevented, health risks avoided, first aid applied and other crises handled.

A standard or operating manual is essential and may take some time to set up. Still, it will assist you in ensuring that there are strict guidelines on how things are done. You can even use these standards to train new staff and as a reference for disciplinary action against those who fail to comply with such standards.

An example of a financial standard is how and when a refund is handled, who has the authority to do refunds, and how the money is refunded to the customer. If you have a risk avoidance standard, it could be how a situation is managed when there's a crucial aspect unavailable and how the customer is treated while the problem persists.

The more standards you have, the better there's a clear understanding of what's expected by your team and customers. These standards should be reviewed annually to ensure they're up-to-date or include new measures that become necessary.

Staff should always be trained on the standards that apply to their position. Remember, you can't have boundaries if you don't have standards.

Control

Standards are what you aspire towards, but they won't guarantee performance. It would help if you created processes to control how your measures are implemented. Written guidelines, product inspection processes, financial checks, and even customer surveys can be effective performance indicators and help you determine if you're meeting your standards.

Processes, procedures, and standards explain how you want your business to operate. For example, a store may wish to:

- put a process in place to achieve sales.
- create mandatory procedures for opening the store.
- set guidelines for how staff dress.
- instruct the quality of customer service required.

Developing processes, procedures, and standards is fundamental if you're in the early stages of establishing your business and also applies when you're trying to grow it. Standards can save you time and money by increasing efficiency. You and your team can get more done quickly by following set processes and procedures.

Standards can also improve the consistency of your products or services. By creating them, you set benchmarks you and your team must meet. For example, you may have a standard for serving customers that involves completing transactions within a specific time and doing everything you can to accommodate customer requests. It will improve your customer's experience. Those customers who have a positive experience are more likely to become repeat customers and less likely to complain about your business.

Implement

Whatever standards you choose, creating processes and procedures for your critical business activities is essential. Depending on the type of business, you may include the following:

- customer service standards
- sales practices and sales policies
- marketing, advertising, and promotion
- staff training and performance reviews
- energy efficiency and environmental considerations
- management responsibilities
- record-keeping and privacy laws
- reporting and cash flow management
- use of technology and mobile phones

For all of your standards to be effective, they must be:

- documented
- grounded in the vision and strategy of your business
- aligned to your values
- clear about general business procedures
- clear about role-specific procedures
- part of your staff training program
- adhered to by you so your team will follow suit
- discussed regularly in meetings
- open to improvement
- designed to empower and inform
- regularly reviewed and updated

You can engage a business adviser or consultant if you need help creating effective procedures, processes, and standards for your business.

CONCLUSION

You want to increase your sales. Unfortunately, there isn't a quick fix that applies to everyone but there are some key strategies to give your business the best chance at thriving.

Scaling your business effectively and efficiently can be difficult, requiring you to think smart and put in the effort. And because you're still a small business, you may wear many hats until you can hire expert staff. Although growing your business will take some time and a lot of energy, there are a few strategies you can use to help accelerate its growth.

- Research is key. When looking into how to grow your business, you need to do market research. It not only lets you understand your existing customers but also potential customers. It's crucial to gain insight into your target market and their needs. That way, you can see how you can meet those needs. Remember to research your competitors, too. Knowing their strengths and weaknesses can help you appropriately scale your business.
- Your sales path can take your business to the next level. Think of a sales path as a customer's journey with you. They're at the top of the path when connecting with your business. They've successfully gone to the other end of the path when they pay for a product or service.

It would help if you tried to find ways to move people through the journey to make a sale. This can include offering a discount, getting their contact details, and sending them updates.

- It's not enough to get new customers for your business. You also need to retain your existing customers. When you do the latter, you're also building customer loyalty, which can increase sales. It costs five times more to get a new customer than to keep a current one. Therefore, focusing on retaining customers means your business will only spend money on something that is a guaranteed investment. You can increase customer retention by:
    - prioritizing customer service
    - using a customer relations management system
    - creating a customer loyalty program
    - launching an email or social media campaign
    - engaging with customers on social media
    - keeping your promises
- Increase your brand's visibility and thus attract new customers and grow your business by participating in networking events. Be bold and attend a few occasions to get people to know about your business. You can participate in such events by:
    - attending and meeting other owners
    - putting up a stall or booth to raise awareness about your business

- - speaking as an industry expert
- Many customers do business with a company that matches their values. Corporate social responsibility means you recognize your business's impact on its environment and community. Letting others see what you're doing to have a positive effect can help your bottom line. Some examples of how your business can do so include:
  - going green by reducing your carbon footprint
  - giving back to the community by volunteering
  - producing healthy and sustainable products
- Sometimes entering into a strategic partnership with another business can give you a chance to reach a broader network of customers. Whatever type of partnership you create, you must manage that relationship and agree to the terms and conditions in writing.
- Diversify your products or services. Suppose you've had success selling your main product or service to customers, and you have the capacity to expand. In that case, consider offering different products or services that can help you get new customers. You can do this by:
  - identifying opportunities for new products or services
  - finding different ways to offer your existing products or services

- Extend your market by considering other markets or even exporting. Finding opportunities means you can ship your products and provide services nationally or even worldwide. The benefits of shipping or virtual services include the following:
    o leveraging national or global platforms to sell your products and services online
    o an opportunity to open new business locations
    o access to more customers and businesses

Measure what works and refine it as you move along. While there are a variety of strategies you can use to grow your small business, you must measure what's working.

As for marketing and sales, be cautious but keep going. Yes, many ways to market your business are out of your reach because you don't have the money, and what works for large corporations won't work for you. But focus on your community and build a presence online.

To grow your small business means you need to take calculated risks. And no matter how small your business is or even if you're an individual service provider, you must have a business plan. It forces you to think clearly about all aspects of your business and make realistic and accurate forecasts of how specific strategies will help you grow your business. Then, regularly monitoring your progress and updating will help you get to where you want to be, namely, running a successful business.

Most people start a business because they either can't find work or they value their personal freedom. In all instances though, what makes you successful isn't the money you make but how you make it. Then it's about what value it adds to your life and those of people in you define as part of your community.

REFERENCES

Ball, J. (2022, May 4). *Council post: The importance of community as a business owner.* Forbes. Retrieved December 11, 2022, from https://www.forbes.com/sites/forbesbusinesscouncil/2022/05/03/the-importance-of-community-as-a-business-owner/

Board, T. A. (n.d.). *8 reasons why your marketing is not working.* Business Advisory Boards and Coaching. Retrieved December 11, 2022, from https://www.thealternativeboard.com/blog/8-reasons-why-your-marketing-is-not-working

Definitions of marketing. American Marketing Association. (2022, July 20). Retrieved December 11, 2022, from https://www.ama.org/the-definition-of-marketing-what-is-marketing/

Hayes, A. (2022, September 15). *Word-of-mouth marketing: Meaning and uses in business.* Investopedia. Retrieved December 11, 2022, from https://www.investopedia.com/terms/w/word-of-mouth-marketing.asp

How to grow a small business in 10 easy steps | the Hartford. (n.d.). Retrieved December 11, 2022, from https://www.thehartford.com/business-insurance/strategy/accelerate-growth/how-to-grow-small-business

The importance of community and Mental Health. NAMI. (n.d.). Retrieved December 11, 2022, from https://nami.org/Blogs/NAMI-Blog/November-

2019/The-Importance-of-Community-and-Mental-Health

Lotich, P. (2022, January 5). *12 steps to implementing a Total Quality Management System.* The Thriving Small Business. Retrieved December 11, 2022, from https://thethrivingsmallbusiness.com/implementing-a-quality-management-system/

Prins, B. (2016). *Insights and tips for owning or managing a hotel.* Amazon. Retrieved December 11, 2022, from https://www.amazon.com/Insights-Tips-Owning-Managing-Hotel/dp/1520149816/

Scott, S. (2022, March 23). *Why word of mouth marketing is important.* Meltwater. Retrieved December 11, 2022, from https://www.meltwater.com/en/blog/word-of-mouth-marketing

Sussex Publishers. (n.d.). *The importance of cultivating community.* Psychology Today. Retrieved December 11, 2022, from https://www.psychologytoday.com/intl/blog/the-flourishing-family/202108/the-importance-cultivating-community

Townsend, C. (2022, January 21). *Why consistency is the key to business success.* The Good Alliance. Retrieved December 11, 2022, from https://thegoodalliance.org/articles/consistency-key-to-business-success/

Verniers, S. (2022, September 8). *Sales techniques: 5 highly effective modern sales methods*. International. Retrieved December 11, 2022, from https://www.teamleader.eu/blog/sales-techniques

What is the definition of sales? - indeed. (n.d.). Retrieved December 11, 2022, from https://www.indeed.com/hire/c/info/definition-of-sales

Why quality matters more than ever in business. GBS Corporate Training. (n.d.). Retrieved December 11, 2022, from https://www.gbscorporate.com/blog/why-quality-matters-more-than-ever-in-business

Williamson, W. (2022, October 7). *Traditional vs contemporary marketing strategies*. Digital Prosperity Blog. Retrieved December 11, 2022, from https://blog.jdrgroup.co.uk/digital-prosperity-blog/traditional-vs-contemporary-marketing-strategies

www.ingramcontent.com/pod-product-compliance
Lightning Source LLC
Chambersburg PA
CBHW071423210526
45465CB00001B/498